Crowned Companion

Expert Secrets to Knowing, Training, and Loving Your Cavalier King Charles Spaniel

CHRISTINE VITOLO

First Stillwater River Publications Edition

ISBN: 978-1-963296-60-0

Library of Congress Control Number: 2024915425

1 2 3 4 5 6 7 8 9 10
Written by Christine Vitolo.
Cover photograph by Stefanie Baum / Adobe Stock.
Title page photograph by Anna Fotyma / Adobe Stock.
Interior photographs & author illustration provided by Christine Vitolo.
Cover & interior book design by Matthew St. Jean.
Published by Stillwater River Publications, West Warwick, RI, USA.

Names: Vitolo, Christine, author.
Title: Crowned companion : expert secrets to knowing, training,
and loving your Cavalier King Charles Spaniel / Christine Vitolo.
Description: First Stillwater River Publications edition. |
West Warwick, RI, USA : Stillwater River Publications, [2024]
Identifiers: ISBN: 978-1-963296-60-0 (paperback) | LCCN: 2024915425
Subjects: LCSH: Cavalier King Charles spaniel--Training. | Cavalier King
Charles spaniel--Health. | Spaniels--Training. | Dogs--Training. | Dog breeds.
Classification: LCC: SF429.C36 V581 2024 | DDC: 636.7524--dc23

CROWNED COMPANION

ALSO BY CHRISTINE VITOLO

The Complete Cavalier Compendium: A Guide to Understanding and Loving Your Cavalier King Charles Spaniel

Knox and Charlie Go to England

Knox and Charlie: The Superhero

Contents

Introduction   *vii*

1   Understanding Your Cavalier King Charles Spaniel   1
2   Socialization, Temperament, and Tailored Training   5
3   The Fundamentals of Positive Reinforcement   7
4   Essential Commands   11
5   Advanced Tricks Training   19
6   House Training and Crate Training   21
7   Addressing Common Behavioral Issues   25
8   Fun and Enrichment Activities   29
9   Health and Wellness   33
10 Training for Specific Roles   39
11 The Aging Cavalier King Charles Spaniel   43

Conclusion   47

Introduction

Welcome to *Crowned Companion: Expert Secrets to Knowing, Training, and Loving Your Cavalier King Charles Spaniel.* This book embarks on an exciting journey to build a strong, loving, and respectful bond between you and your regal friend through training. Renowned for their affectionate nature, intelligence, and graceful demeanor, Cavaliers have earned their place as one of the world's most beloved and sought-after companion dogs.

Throughout this book, we delve into the art and science of nurturing a relationship with these graceful dogs through effective and positive training methods. Recognized for their affectionate nature and eagerness to please, Cavaliers possess an innate intelligence that allows them to excel in various roles, from being loyal family companions to adept therapy dogs or even successful show performers.

Each chapter will explore the intricacies of understanding the Cavalier King Charles Spaniel's unique personality and communication style. Delving into their mindset, we will build a foundation of trust, respect, and loyalty. This deep connection enables us to unlock their true potential and create a partnership based on love and cooperation.

The first section of this book traces the history and origins of the Cavalier King Charles Spaniel, from their lineage in the royal courts of England to their esteemed status as beloved companions. Understanding their heritage deepens appreciation for the breed and provides valuable insights into their behavior and instincts.

Subsequent chapters will introduce the fundamental principles of training the Cavalier with a compassionate and positive approach. We highlight the significance of reward-based training, using praise, treats, and affection to reinforce desired behaviors without the use of aversive methods or punishment. Moreover, we address common training challenges with patience and guidance.

Beyond basic obedience, we explore the world of canine sports and activities ideally suited for the enthusiastic spirit of this breed. From agility and rally obedience to nose work and therapy dog programs, Cavaliers always exhibit an uncanny ability to shine, providing rewarding adventures that foster growth and fulfillment.

In addition, we emphasize the importance of health and care in raising a Cavalier King Charles Spaniel. With their specific health considerations, we offer comprehensive guidance on nutrition, exercise, grooming, and preventive measures to ensure your companion's well-being and longevity.

Throughout this book, we aim to equip you with a comprehensive toolkit that encompasses training techniques and an appreciation for the partnership you will forge. With patience, kindness, and consistency, you will unlock the full potential of your noble companion.

Whether you are a first-time owner or an experienced dog lover, *Crowned Companion: Expert Secrets to Knowing, Training, and Loing Your Cavalier King Charles Spaniel* will guide you in cultivating a lifelong relationship with this gentle and loving being.

1 Understanding Your Cavalier King Charles Spaniel

In this chapter, we delve into the history and origins of the Cavalier King Charles Spaniel breed, as understanding their roots allows us to comprehend their inherent traits and behavior patterns. The Cavalier King Charles Spaniel is known for its regal appearance, affectionate nature, and history that dates back centuries. Their roots are interwoven with royalty, companionship, and love, making them cherished companions for countless families across the globe. With this in mind, we look to the past to better adapt our training methods to this unique breed.

Origins

The origins of the Cavalier King Charles Spaniel can be traced back to the seventeenth century in England. The breed is believed to have descended from small toy spaniels that were popular among European nobility during the Renaissance era. The first recorded mention of a Cavalier King Charles Spaniel dates back to the sixteenth century when Mary, Queen of Scots, was said to have owned a small spaniel named Puss. These early toy spaniels were favored companions of the aristocracy and were often depicted in the paintings of renowned artists such as Titian and Van Dyck. The breed's association with royalty continued, and they became particularly favored during the reign of King Charles II in the seventeenth century, after

whom they were named. It's important to note that these adorable Spaniels were not exclusive to the aristocracy; they also found their way into the hearts and homes of common folk, endearing themselves as beloved companions across various social classes. The breed's history is rich and diverse, reflecting its appeal to individuals from all walks of life in historic England.

The late nineteenth century was a transformative period for the Cavalier King Charles Spaniel breed. During this era, dog breeding practices experienced a significant shift as breeders began to standardize their techniques and focus on preserving specific traits. This shift ultimately altered the breed's appearance through crossbreeding with other toy breeds like the Pug and Japanese Chin. As a result, the Cavalier King Charles Spaniel started to exhibit a flatter head and a shorter nose, distinguishing it from its earlier counterparts. Some breeders found these changes appealing and referred to the resulting dogs as "King Charles Spaniels."

Nevertheless, amidst these changes, a group of passionate enthusiasts, spearheaded by an American named Roswell Eldridge, sought to revive the original look of the breed as depicted in historical paintings. Eldridge, driven by his dedication to preserving the breed's traditional form, decided to take action. In 1926, he offered a generous cash prize at the prestigious Crufts

Hendrick Danckerts, *Royal Gardener John Rose presenting a pineappel* [sic] *to King Charles II*, 1675

Dog Show to any breeder capable of producing a dog that closely resembled the authentic Cavalier King Charles Spaniel. This bold and visionary initiative began extensive efforts to re-establish the breed's pure and authentic glory as we recognize it today.

The prize offered by Roswell Eldridge was not merely a financial incentive but a rallying call for breeders to unite in pursuing this noble endeavor. His vision was rooted in a genuine appreciation for the breed's historical significance and a desire to honor its heritage. The competition at Crufts Dog Show spurred breeders to delve into the breed's past and understand its origins, allowing them to comprehend the specific characteristics that made the original Cavalier King Charles Spaniel truly unique.

The revitalization efforts were not without their challenges, as breeders had to navigate a complex web of genetic traits and carefully select breeding pairs to achieve the desired results. Striving to reverse the effects of the previous crossbreeding and restore the breed's classic features was no easy task. However, the enthusiasts' dedication and unwavering commitment to the breed's essence ultimately triumphed. Breeders recreated the quintessential Cavalier King Charles Spaniel through careful and thoughtful breeding practices. This revived version of the breed captured the hearts of dog lovers worldwide, attracting admiration for its graceful appearance and gentle temperament.

As the years passed, the Cavalier King Charles Spaniel established itself as a beloved companion animal whose resurgence reinforced the importance of preserving purebred lines and respecting the historical heritage of dog breeds.

Today, the Cavalier King Charles Spaniel is a testament to the power of passionate dedication and responsible breeding practices. Its captivating appearance and endearing personality make it a favored choice among dog owners seeking a faithful and loving companion. Thanks to the visionary efforts of individuals like Roswell Eldridge and the united commitment of breeders, this charming little Spaniel continues to flourish and enchant generations of dog lovers worldwide.

Inherent Traits, Characteristics, and Behavior Patterns

The Cavalier King Charles Spaniel possesses a set of exceptional traits that contribute to its immense popularity as a cherished pet. These characteristics can be categorized as follows:

Adaptability: Adaptable and versatile, Cavaliers effortlessly adjust to diverse environments. Their contentment in bustling cities or quiet countryside homes coupled with their small size and easygoing temperament makes them particularly well-suited for apartment living.

Adequate exercise and mental stimulation are important components for maintaining their well-being.

Compatibility with Other Pets: Among their many exceptional qualities, the Cavalier's ability to coexist harmoniously with other animals stands out. Naturally sociable, they form amicable relationships not only with other dogs but also with cats. This congenial nature reflects their historical role as valued companions and lapdogs.

Aesthetic Appeal: The enduring popularity of the Cavalier King Charles Spaniel can be attributed, in part, to their striking appearance. Distinctive features, such as a sweet and expressive face adorned with large, dark, soulful eyes complemented by a silky, feathered coat showcasing colors like tricolor, Blenheim, black and tan, and ruby contribute to the breed's overall aesthetic appeal. Physical traits like a plume-like tail and long, soft ears add to their visual allure.

Loyalty and Devotion: Beneath their beauty lies a loyal and devoted nature. Cavaliers form deep bonds with their owners, thriving on human companionship. Their eagerness to please makes training sessions enjoyable and effective. Their intelligence and willingness to learn further contribute to their overall appeal as pets.

Training: Despite their inherent amiability, Cavaliers require proper training and socialization to develop into well-rounded and polite pets. While generally social, they may be reserved around strangers. Early socialization

amiable temperament, Cavaliers are highly social dogs that love interacting with people and other animals. This sociable nature can be harnessed during training, making them receptive to learning new commands.

Behavior Patterns and Hunting Instincts: The Cavalier King Charles Spaniel is renowned for its friendly and sociable nature, endearing itself to many as a warm companion. Beyond separation anxiety and prey drive, additional behavioral traits, such as barking and leash pulling, may surface, rooted in their breeding history linked to hunting. Understanding these characteristics provides valuable insights for pet owners in addressing and managing these behaviors.

Another aspect of the Cavalier's behavior stems from their hunting heritage, instilling an instinctual drive to pursue small animals and birds. While not inherently harmful, this behavior can be problematic if not addressed. Recall training—teaching the dog to come when called—becomes invaluable to manage these pursuits.

The Cavalier King Charles Spaniel's behavioral patterns are influenced by their inherent loyalty to their human family and their historical role as hunting companions. Understanding tendencies, such as potential separation anxiety and the instinct to chase small animals, is vital for responsible owners. Patient training from an early age, including recall training and socialization, helps create a well-adjusted and content Cavalier capable of enjoying a safe and happy life alongside their human companions.

is essential to prevent undesirable traits from emerging, aiding young dogs in becoming more confident and well-adjusted adults.

Grooming and Physical Activity: Maintaining the beauty and health of the Cavalier's coat is a near-daily event, necessitating regular grooming practices. Brushing their fur fosters a meaningful bonding experience between the dog and its owner. Scheduled grooming appointments or haircuts along with at-home upkeep are necessary for optimal coat condition. While not demanding intense physical activity, daily walks and playtime contribute to both mental and physical stimulation, promoting overall happiness and preventing behavioral issues.

Understanding Nature for Effective Training: Before delving into training techniques, understanding the nature of the Cavalier King Charles Spaniel is essential. Known for their gentle and

2   Socialization, Temperament, and Tailored Training

The process of socialization is a pivotal aspect of nurturing a well-rounded and confident Cavalier King Charles Spaniel. This involves exposing your pup to a variety of experiences in a positive and controlled manner, shaping their behavior and outlook on the world. Early socialization is fundamental for fostering the charming and affectionate nature that defines the breed, ensuring they thrive in social interactions throughout their life.

1. Early Socialization

Early interaction plays a critical role in the development of a well-adjusted and confident dog. This process unfolds between the third and twelfth weeks of life, a period when the puppy is highly receptive to novel experiences. The objective is to minimize the likelihood of fear, anxiety, or aggression in the future, encouraging a confident and relaxed demeanor in the presence of unfamiliar stimuli.

2. Exposure to People

Introducing your Cavalier King Charles Spaniel to diverse groups of people is vital for their socialization. Expose them to individuals of varying ages, ethnicities, and appearances to ensure they remain comfortable and amicable around strangers. Encourage gentle interactions and reward positive responses, establishing a strong foundation for approaching new people with curiosity and confidence. The ultimate goal is for the dog to act neutrally to all people—neither pulling on the leash to say hello nor shrinking away. The dog should always remain focused on the handler, even in a crowd.

3. Interaction with Other Animals

Another component of socialization is acquainting the puppy with other animals. Facilitate controlled and supervised introductions with fellow dogs, cats, and other household pets. It is often a good idea to keep the puppy on a leash or use some kind of physical boundary for the first introduction. Positive experiences with other creatures help build social skills and encourage harmonious relationships, especially in multi-pet households. Once again, the goal is neutrality around other animals, with the dog neither pulling at the leash nor shrinking away.

4. Environmental Exposure and Novel Objects

Exposure to different environments and novel objects is equally important for developing a well-rounded Cavalier King Charles Spaniel. Introduce them to various indoor and outdoor settings, diverse sounds, textures, smells, and even weather. Some puppies can be a little nervous

in the wind or rain, especially with leaves blowing around their face. This fosters adaptability and minimizes anxiety when faced with new surroundings later in life, making them more adaptable and well-adjusted pets. Training in different environments, like parks, stores, the sidewalk, and homes helps to desensitize a dog to new stimuli.

Individual Variations for Tailored Training Techniques

When engaging in the socialization process, advance at the dog's pace, avoiding overwhelming them with excessive stimuli. Patience and consistency are critical, especially during developmental fear phases. Tailor the training to the individual pup, considering their unique temperament and comfort levels. This ensures that encounters are not only positive but also free from unnecessary stress.

It's important to acknowledge individual variations in temperament within the breed.

Some Cavaliers may exhibit shyness or reserved behavior, emphasizing the importance of consistent socialization efforts during their formative weeks. Addressing maladaptive social behavior should involve consultation with a certified trainer to rectify specific issues.

While the breed's friendly and affectionate nature makes them excellent companions, Cavaliers may not be well-suited for guard dog roles. Their inclination towards warmth and curiosity rather than hostility means they are less likely to display aggression towards strangers.

It is always worth reminding yourself that every dog is different, just as every person is different. For example, more reserved dogs will need to be exposed to stimuli at a slower pace and with more repetition in order to build confidence over a period of time.

Socialization is more than just exposing a dog to new stimuli, it is also about actively working to create a positive association with that stimuli using treats and praise.

3 The Fundamentals of Positive Reinforcement

As the art and science of dog training have evolved over many years, positive reinforcement has consistently emerged as the key to unlocking the potential of our beloved companions. This chapter will delve into the fundamentals of positive reinforcement training, empowering you to effectively utilize rewards, praise, and encouragement to mold desired behaviors in your Cavalier King Charles Spaniel. From mastering basic commands to embarking on the journey of advanced tricks, positive reinforcement will pave the way for a rewarding and joyous training experience for you and your four-legged friend.

Understanding Positive Reinforcement

Positive reinforcement is a training technique centered on rewarding desired behaviors, thereby increasing the likelihood of their repetition. This approach involves creating positive associations with specific people, environments, objects, and various stimuli, fostering the dog's eagerness to perform certain behaviors in anticipation of rewards. For Cavalier King Charles Spaniels, known for thriving on affection and bonding, positive reinforcement proves particularly effective in cultivating a deep connection between the owner and the pet. Scientifically, observable effects of positive reinforcement

include promoting calm and settled behaviors, reducing stress-related actions, and enhancing the dog's willingness to engage in training. The measurable differences brought about by positive reinforcement not only strengthen the owner-pet bond but also contribute to the overall well-being and positive behavior of the Cavalier.

Choosing the Right Rewards

Beginning positive reinforcement training with your Cavalier King Charles Spaniel necessitates a thoughtful selection of rewards. Opt for high value treats like small pieces of chicken, cheese, or liver, as these serve as potent motivators, particularly during initial training sessions. It's worth mentioning that commonly labeled "training treats" may not be high value for most dogs and might not be suitable for more distracting or challenging environments, such as group classes or outdoor settings. As your dog gains proficiency, there is room to gradually transition to lower value treats or even verbal praise, affection, and eye contact can become effective rewards. Always remember that any attention, good or bad, can be considered rewarding if a dog is misbehaving in order to try and get that attention. Consideration of the dog's preferred training time—be it after exercise or before a meal—and the training environment—whether in the living room, outdoors, or in different lesson settings—can impact the efficacy of specific rewards. Understanding how a dog's preferences align with the owner's choice of rewards plays a valuable role in shaping successful training outcomes.

Contra Feeding

The scientific concept of contra feeding challenges the conventional belief that animals, including the food-motivated Cavalier King Charles Spaniel, prefer obtaining their meals with minimal effort. Contrary to this notion, contra feeding proposes that animals may find greater satisfaction in working for their food. For these dogs, known for their high food motivation, integrating training sessions into mealtime can prove to be an effective strategy. This may involve activities such as having the dog sit before meals, placing kibble in puzzle toys or roller balls, or using a snuffle mat to engage their mental and physical faculties. By incorporating mental stimulation into mealtime activities, not only do you cater to their love for food, but you also address the risk of obesity—a common concern in this breed exacerbated by calorie-rich expressions of human affection. Contra feeding not only positively impacts obesity but also serves as an enriching measure, mitigating boredom and fostering a balanced and fulfilling relationship with food.

Timing is Everything

The timing of reinforcement is an important part of positive reinforcement training. Immediate rewards ensure that your dog associates the treat or praise directly with the performed behavior, thereby preventing confusion and strengthening the positive reinforcement association. An easy and effective way to incorporate precise timing into training is through clicker training.

Clicker training utilizes a handheld device—known as a clicker—to enhance canine learning rooted in operant conditioning, a method focused on cause and effect rather than punitive consequences. Key principles include the clicker serving as a precise marker signal, indicating precisely when the dog has exhibited the desired behavior. The click occurs immediately after the desired action, fostering a clear association. Positive reinforcement is fundamental, pairing the clicker with an immediate reward, often a treat, creating a positive association and encouraging behavior repetition. Consistency in marking and rewarding desired behaviors reinforces expectations. It typically takes ten to fifteen repetitions to create an association, with a critical timeframe of two seconds for marking the performed behavior, ensuring a quick association.

Studies suggest that using a clicker aids in increasing dogs' confidence, as the distinct, brief sound it produces remains audible even in busier or distracting environments. The philosophy of clicker training revolves around a no-punishment approach, focusing on reinforcing and shaping desired behaviors. This method establishes clear communication, with the click precisely signaling the moment of the behavior, eliminating confusion. For dogs, confusion can result in stress and frustration. The training is designed to be enjoyable and engaging, turning the dog into an active participant and fostering a positive learning experience that enhances their willingness to cooperate.

4 Essential Commands

Basic Commands Training

Training a well-behaved Cavalier King Charles Spaniel is essential to responsible pet ownership. These charming and affectionate dogs thrive in a loving environment and enjoy pleasing their owners. It's important to teach them fundamental commands to establish a strong bond and maintain a well-behaved pet. In this comprehensive guide, we will explore step-by-step training techniques for essential commands providing you with the knowledge and tools to achieve impressive results consistently and patiently.

Loading the Clicker

Before we start anything, we have to talk about loading the clicker. The clicker should be used on every single cue to aid the training commands. It helps the dog learn faster, focus through distractions, and is scientifically proven to get better results. All you have to do is click and then immediately treat your dog ten times in a row. Wait for your dog to look away, then click again. They should turn back in anticipation of getting a treat. Practice this ten times until it becomes second nature.

1. Look

This is all about eye contact and focus on the handler. If you have your dog's eyes/attention, you have their whole world. We often use "Look"

to refocus a dog who may be reactive, nervous/unsure, or simply distracted. My dog used to be afraid of school buses, so whenever one passed, I would have her look at me, and I'd give her a bunch of treats. She is no longer afraid of buses and routinely looks at me for a treat when they drive by. The "Look" cue is great for helping

dogs build positive associations to stimuli and get over their fears.

When teaching this you should be standing up straight. Bending over the dog can be seen as intimidating and your dog is actually less likely to make eye contact with you. Also, some people like to use "Focus" or "Watch me" as the verbal cue instead of "Look."

First, bring a treat from right in front of your dog's nose (practically touching their nose) in a straight line to your nose. When the dog makes eye contact, click and treat. Practice this ten to fifteen times.

Next, you're replacing the treat with your index finger. You're drawing a line with your pointer finger from in front of their nose to yours. Click and treat for eye contact. Practice this ten times.

When your dog is reliably giving you eye contact, you can start asking them to "Look" when you use your hand cue (pointing from their nose to yours). Continue clicking and treating for eye contact.

2. Sit

The "Sit" command stands as one of the initial and essential behaviors to impart to your Cavalier King Charles Spaniel. It serves as the cornerstone for obedience and contributes to managing their behavior in diverse situations. Teaching the "Sit" command establishes a fundamental aspect of doggy manners, promoting politeness in your pet. We like to say that Sitting is your dog's way of saying "please." They should Sit for treats, meals, waiting at doors, greeting strangers, etc.

"Sit" and "Look" are super helpful for puppies when they go on walks and decide they don't want to go any further. It typically means the puppy is a bit overwhelmed and wants to return closer to home. We recommend just having the puppy do Sits and Looks for a bit until they feel comfortable enough with the environment to continue the walk.

Begin by holding a treat near your Cavalier King Charles Spaniel's nose, then gradually elevate your hand, guiding the dog's attention upwards and slightly backwards over their head. As your pup follows the treat, its rear end will naturally lower to the ground. Once in the seated position, click and treat to promptly reward your dog with the treat and offer enthusiastic praise. Over time, transition from using the lure to responding to a hand cue. Introduce the verbal command "Sit" once your dog consistently performs the action in response to the hand cue. Conduct short practice sessions (five minutes, five to ten times a day), gradually diminishing the reliance on treats while introducing verbal praise and physical affection as alternative forms of reinforcement. This step-by-step approach ensures a smooth transition from treat-based guidance to a command that can be executed with verbal cues and positive interactions.

Remember to introduce this cue by utilizing the clicker from the get-go. Encourage your Cavalier King Charles Spaniel to Sit by gently guiding them with a treat, clicking at the moment their hindquarters touch the ground. Swiftly follow the click with a treat and praise, reinforcing the association between the action and positive reinforcement. Regular practice of the "Sit" command not only cultivates good manners but also establishes a solid foundation for further training and positive behavior in your Cavalier King Charles Spaniel.

3. Down

The "Down" cue in dog training serves as a fundamental command to encourage a dog to lower its body and lie down. This command involves not only the front part of the dog's body but also emphasizes the importance of gently flopping over the back hips. This deliberate positioning helps foster a more settled mindset, preventing the dog from impulsively pouncing up. To train this behavior effectively, start by placing the dog in the Sit position and lure them to the floor with a treat brought from their nose straight down to ground level. Once the dog's belly is touching the floor, encourage the dog to flop their hips over by moving the treat in an arc to their hip. In order to better reach the treat, the dog will likely reposition themselves by turning their hips to one side into a more relaxed position.

Click at the precise moment the hips flop over, reinforcing the desired behavior with a treat. Subsequently, gradually incorporate the "Down" cue with the clicker during practice sessions, emphasizing the importance of the hip flop for a calm and controlled response. This approach ensures a clear association between the cue, the behavior, and the positive reinforcement, creating a well-established and reliable response to the "Down" command. Remember to incorporate the clicker from the beginning. The clarity the clicker provides makes it much easier for the puppy to learn what is being asked of them.

4. Stay

Establishing the "Stay" command is both for the safety and discipline of your Cavalier King Charles Spaniel. Commence by instructing your dog to Sit, and with your palm facing outward, issue the command "Stay" as you take a step backward.

Swiftly return to your starting position in front of the dog. If your dog maintained the Stay, click and treat and then give them the Release cue, "Release!" Your dog only gets treats when they are still in the Stay position before being Released. They get nothing for the Release.

Typically, we allow any dog in a Stay to get more comfortable, going from a Sit to a Down, but not the other way around.

If your dog broke the Stay, give them their Release cue when they first get up and simply begin again by asking them to Stay. If your dog is Releasing themselves often, you are progressing too quickly— either walking too far away or waiting too long to return. When your dog Releases themself, say "Release!" and turn your back on them for five to ten seconds.

It is helpful to practice breaking eye contact with your dog when they are in a Stay. If you're always looking at them, they can interpret a break in eye contact as a Release cue. Make sure to turn your head, even your whole body at times.

Immediately reward your pup if they successfully maintain the sitting position. Gradually increase both the distance and duration of the Stay while consistently reinforcing adherence. Introducing a Release cue is equally important, signaling the end of the behavior. Focus on initially building duration and then distance for a more comprehensive "Stay" command. Remember that rewards for Staying are always provided directly in front of the dog, emphasizing the importance of the owner's return. Employ the simile of going away and "snapping back" like a rubber band, reinforcing the Stay position with a click and treat upon return. The Release itself holds no reward, creating a clear distinction. After the Release, restart the training cycle by asking your dog to stay once again. A Down Stay is a fundamental command for a calm, settled dog and should be practiced often in environments with varying levels of distraction/difficulty.

5. Come

The "Come" command is needed for ensuring the safety of your Cavalier, teaching them

Practicing the "Stay" command

to return to you promptly, even in potentially hazardous situations. Follow this step-by-step training technique to instill this essential command. To reinforce this command with your Cavalier King Charles Spaniel, equip yourself with a treat, squat down, and call your dog's name enthusiastically followed by the "Come" command. As your dog approaches, reward it generously with treats and affection, creating positive associations with the Recall.

Start with very small distances—perhaps one step away. Hold a treat between your knees as a lure so that the dog Comes right in front of you. Ideally, the dog would Recall directly in front of you, not just your general vicinity, so that way you can grab them quickly if needed and they can't just bounce away. Consider incorporating grabbing the dog's collar as part of the cue so that the dog doesn't jump away when you try to catch them. For example, clicking and treating with one hand and patting/grabbing with the other.

A good tip is to stare directly at the ground in front of your feet where you want your dog to Recall to. Eye contact is a reward, and the dog will want to come over and stand where you are staring. Another tip is to be mindful of when you are asking your dog to Recall. Many people only Recall their dog to be put back on leash to leave the park, and the Recall becomes a signal to the dog that the fun is over. Routinely ask your dog to Recall, click and treat, and then Release them back to more fun. This way, Recall is a highly rewarding quick check in with you and not always a signal the fun is ending.

Regularly practice the "Come" command in a secure and controlled environment, initially re-lying on the leash for safety. Most pet stores now sell extra-long leashes which can be very helpful. Gradually reduce reliance on the leash by practicing in a fenced enclosure, ensuring a gradual transition toward off-leash reliability. This approach reinforces a strong Recall response, enhancing the safety and well-being of your Cavalier. High-value treats are always a good approach to training, particularly in distracting environments where the temptation to ignore the Recall may be stronger. By incorporating these elements, you enhance the effectiveness of the "Come" command and promote a reliable response from your Cavalier King Charles Spaniel.

6. Take It

Hold a treat in your hand and wave it up and down repeatedly in front of your dog. When your dog shows self-control (in one of three ways), click and treat, and tell them "Take It." Practice this ten times.

Ways a dog can show self-control:

1. Looking away from the treat. (They are not staring at the treat and look elsewhere.)
2. Sitting or laying down. (Sitting is how they say please.)
3. Moving away from the treat/giving you space.

When the dog is reliably showing self-control, make it a bit harder. Hold the treat in your hand in a fist in front of the dog. If the dog is showing self-control (in one of the above three ways) for five whole seconds, click and treat and tell them "Take It." Usually we deliver the treat to the dog's mouth, but for Take It, we want the dog coming into our space and taking the treat. If the dog moves toward the treat to eat it, close your fist, and wait for them to show self-control. Then the five second countdown begins again. As your dog progresses, hold your hand lower to the ground so that your dog will need to exercise even more impulse control before being allowed to Take It.

7. Leave It

The "Leave It" command plays a pivotal role in your dog's safety by preventing them from picking up harmful items or consuming potentially dangerous substances. This command is particularly important in avoiding instances where dogs may encounter common hazards such as toxic foods, sharp objects, or harmful chemicals. Utilizing the "Leave It" command helps instill a vital skill that safeguards your dog from potential dangers in their environment.

We often use less smelly/appetizing treats (like a milk bone) as the "poison cookie." That way, if the dog eats it, no harm is done, and we are not making their lives harder by telling them they can't have a delicious, smellier treat.

Having success with timing for Leave It involves setting yourself up to deliver the reward treat before you toss down the poison cookie. I recommend having the poison cookie in one hand and the clicker/reward treat in the other hand.

Drop the poison cookie on the ground and loosely cover it with a hand cage. Wait for the dog to show self-control in one of the three ways. When your dog is showing self-control, click and toss the reward treat a bit away off to the side so the dog has to go get it. Take up the poison cookie and wait for the dog to return. Drop the poison cookie, hand cage, and begin again.

When the puppy is reliably showing self-control, you can then ask them to Leave It before clicking and treating.

As the dog progresses, hold your hand above the poison cookie farther and farther away. If the dog is able to snatch and eat the poison, you're progressing too quickly and not holding your hand close enough to block the poison if needed.

Increase your distance away from the poison cookie as the dog shows more and more self-control. Always pick up the poison in between rounds.

Practice the Leave It command with various objects and treats, progressively advancing to more challenging items, reinforcing the skill, and promoting a reliable response from your dog.

It's important to note that Take It and Leave It should not be practiced simultaneously, as the latter is specifically designed for items your dog should never have, such as grapes, wires, or shoes. By dedicating separate sessions to each command, you effectively build a solid foundation for impulse control in your Cavalier King Charles Spaniel.

8. Loose Leash Walking

Loose leash walking is a fundamental skill in training. This cue teaches a dog to walk calmly and closely beside the owner without pulling on the leash. It promotes an enjoyable walking experience for both the dog and the owner. To establish this behavior, consistent reinforcement and positive rewards are key. The goal is for the dog to learn to match their pace with the handler, fostering a connection and enhancing the overall walking relationship. Teaching loose leash walking not only ensures a more pleasant stroll but also reinforces the importance of communication and cooperation between the dog and its owner.

The dog is allowed to be a bit in front of you or off to the side as long as there is slack in the leash and they're not pulling. We recommend you choose a side to walk your dog on, left or right, as this will simplify things greatly. Opposite to the side your dog is on, have the leash up above your elbow and hold the clicker. The hand on the same side as the dog is going to be delivering treats. Always give your dog the same amount of leash to work with. If you hold it short one day and give them more slack the next, they will get confused about how far away they should be from you. Consistency is better.

Start with your dog next to you and tell them "Let's Go," which means start walking. As long as your dog is not pulling, you are clicking and treating. You repeat "Let's Go," clicking and treating very often (every two or so steps, almost continuously at first). If your dog pulls, you stop moving immediately. Forward motion is its own reward for a dog. Wait for your dog to check in with you, then lure them back to your side with a treat and begin again. They get nothing for returning to you; they only get a treat after they have been walking nicely by your side again. Otherwise, they learn that if they pull, when they return, they'll get a treat. .

Remember, consistency and patience are key elements in successful training. Using the step-by-step techniques discussed above, you can teach your companion essential commands such as sit, stay, come, heel, and leave it, ensuring their safety, good manners, and enjoyable interactions with humans and other animals.

As you embark on this training journey with your Cavalier, remember that positive reinforcement and love are powerful motivators. Celebrate each milestone, no matter how small, and embrace the joy of watching your friend grow into a well-behaved and delightful companion. Happy training!

5   Advanced Tricks Training

Advanced trick training for dogs extends well beyond the basics, offering numerous advantages for both the pet and the owner. Going beyond essential commands not only enhances a dog's physical coordination but also stimulates their mental acuity. Engaging in advanced tricks provides an avenue for continuous learning, reinforcing the bond between the dog and its owner. It instills a sense of achievement and boosts the dog's confidence, showcasing their intelligence and adaptability. Beyond the practical benefits, advanced tricks serve as an outlet for creativity and play, transforming training sessions into enjoyable and interactive experiences. This ongoing commitment to training past the essentials not only nurtures a well-rounded and mentally stimulated canine companion but also reinforces the unique partnership between the dog and its owner. Remember to always use the clicker to enhance the training commands and reward your dog.

1. Roll Over

Instructing your dog to execute a rollover is both delightful and impressive. Begin with your dog in a Down position and entice them with a treat held close to their nose. Gradually move the treat in an arc over to the other side of the dog, behind their shoulder, encouraging them to turn their head and then their entire body to follow the treat. As your Cavalier King Charles Spaniel accomplishes the roll, reward them with the treat and shower them with praise.

2. Spin

The "Spin" trick adds a fun and whimsical element to your dog's repertoire. Start with your dog standing in front of you. With a treat in hand, lead it in a circular motion around its head, guiding it to turn in the same direction. Upon completing the Spin, reward your dog and repeat the process to reinforce the trick. The circular motion must be very wide, enough to accommodate the dog's whole body.

3. Heel

This trick uses similar mechanics to loose leash walking, but instead of saying "Let's Go," you're telling your dog "Heel." Start with your dog by your side so that their nose is in line with the seam of your pants. You want your dog to maintain this position at your side, no wandering ahead, etc. Tell your dog "Heel" and begin walking. Use a treat as a lure to keep your dog's head right where you want them. Click and treat as your dog holds the position while walking. If they wander or pull on the leash, get them back in position and start again (just like loose leash walking). Practice inside and outside turns with your dog maintaining their Heel position. Fade the lure over time.

6   House Training and Crate Training

House- and crate training are essential aspects of responsible pet ownership, particularly for Cavalier King Charles Spaniels. These affectionate dogs make wonderful companions but require patience, consistency, and understanding during training. This chapter will explore how to successfully house- and crate train your Cavalier King Charles Spaniel, ensuring a clean and comfortable living environment for you and your companion. Proper house training establishes the foundation for a well-behaved and well-adjusted dog. It ensures your home remains clean, odor-free, and harmonious while also establishing a clear communication channel between you and your pet, fostering trust and understanding.

Dealing with Potty Accidents

Accidents are an inevitable part of the house-training process. When accidents happen, responding calmly and avoiding punishing your dog is essential. Punishment can create fear and anxiety, making training more challenging. Dogs who have been punished for accidents will often start hiding their accidents or even eating their waste, which is not good for anyone.

To initiate crate training, begin by introducing the dog to the crate as a positive and safe space. Gradually acclimate them by placing treats and toys, allowing them to associate the crate with positive experiences. Over time, increase the duration they spend inside, always ensuring it remains a positive experience.

First, the door should stay open so they can come and go as they please. Then the door is closed very briefly. This duration increases at the dog's pace. Next, the door should be closed, and the owner briefly steps out of the room (five to ten seconds) and returns calmly and quietly. Lastly, the duration of time with the crate door closed and owner out of the room increases.

Dogs should also have cues to go in and exit the crate. The puppy should be in a Down position, calm and settled, before being told to exit. The puppy is ignored if they are whining/barking and only let out when they are calm.

The benefits of crate training, especially for dogs with separation anxiety, are noteworthy. The confined space provides a sense of security, akin to a den, reducing anxiety levels. Additionally, it establishes a routine and a designated space, offering comfort and stability in the dog's world. Crate training can be a powerful tool in managing separation anxiety, providing a retreat where the dog feels protected, and easing the stress associated with being alone. Regular reinforcement ensures that the crate becomes a cherished sanctuary for the dog.

No matter the route you choose for separation training, it is essential to make the process positive and rewarding. Owners can start by leaving the room for just a few minutes, gradually increasing the duration over time. Engaging

with toys or treats can help distract the dog and create positive associations with being alone. Additionally, establishing a consistent departure routine can signal to the dog that absences are temporary and not a cause for concern.

Supervision and Confinement for Accident Prevention

Maintaining close supervision indoors is essential to prevent accidents. Utilize baby gates or keep your Cavalier in the same room as you. When direct supervision is not possible, consider crate training as a safe and effective method to manage behavior. Frequent potty accidents may indicate the need to gradually limit their freedom. A consistent daily crate training schedule for potty training intervals reinforces positive habits and aids in overall house-training success.

Crate Training: A Secure Haven

Crate training is an effective approach, offering your Cavalier a secure haven where they can retreat and feel at ease. When executed properly, crate training becomes a positive experience. Beyond house training, crates offer benefits during overnight stays at the vet, evacuation scenarios, or resting after an injury. Encourage continued crate use throughout adulthood for a consistent and comforting retreat.

Choosing the Right Crate

Select an appropriately sized crate, allowing your Cavalier to stand, turn around, and lie down comfortably. Avoid choosing a crate that is too large, as this might lead to the dog using one end as a bathroom.

Introduction to the Crate

Introduce the crate gradually and positively. Place treats, toys, and familiar bedding inside to make it inviting. Allow your Cavalier to explore the crate at their own pace, avoiding any attempts to force them inside. Keep the crate door open initially, ensuring a positive and stress-free introduction to their new space.

Positive Association with the Crate

Establish a positive association by providing treats and praise when your dog willingly enters the crate. Avoid using the crate as punishment, as this can create negative associations. Gradually desensitize your dog to the closed crate door, starting with short intervals and extending the time with positive reinforcement.

Gradual Alone Time

Once comfortable with the crate, leave your Cavalier alone for short periods, gradually increasing the duration as they exhibit calmness. Start with short intervals and progress to longer durations, ensuring a positive and gradual acclimation to being alone in the crate.

Using the Crate for House-Training

Incorporate crate training during house-training to prevent indoor accidents. Avoid leaving your Cavalier in the crate for excessively long periods to prevent anxiety. Adjust the duration based on age and bladder control. Thoroughly clean up accidents to eliminate odors, discouraging repeat incidents.

Observing Patterns and Adjusting Routine

Observe your Cavalier's behavior to establish potty schedule patterns. Adjust the schedule if accidents persist, taking your dog out more frequently to prevent holding it too long.

Establishing a Routine

Creating a consistent routine is key to successful house-training. Take your Cavalier outside to the designated potty area regularly throughout the day. Puppies have smaller bladders and will need to relieve themselves more frequently. Generally, take your puppy out first thing in the morning, after meals, playtime, and before bedtime. Adult dogs can generally wait longer between potty breaks. Dogs should not be expected to hold their bladder any longer than six hours.

7   Addressing Common Behavioral Issues

Cavalier King Charles Spaniels are beloved for their friendly nature, making them wonderful companions. However, like any dog breed, Cavaliers may develop specific behavioral issues that can be challenging for the dog and its owner. Three common behavioral problems faced by Cavalier King Charles Spaniel owners are separation anxiety, excessive barking, and leash pulling. This comprehensive guide will delve into the root causes of these issues and explore proven training techniques to help your Cavalier overcome these obstacles and develop a more balanced demeanor.

1. Understanding Separation Anxiety

Separation anxiety is a common behavioral issue that affects many dogs, including Cavaliers. This condition occurs when a dog becomes excessively distressed or anxious when left alone, often leading to destructive behaviors such as chewing, scratching, or excessive vocalization. Understanding the triggers behind separation anxiety helps to address the problem effectively.

Causes of Separation Anxiety

Cavaliers are affectionate dogs that thrive on companionship and yearn to form deep bonds with their human family members. It's important to note that feelings of abandonment and anxiety, particularly when left alone, are not necessarily indicative of the strength of that bond, which has been a common myth for years. Separation anxiety is more closely linked to a disposition for anxiety and a lack of early training rather than how attached they are. Proper training and addressing anxiety-related tendencies can contribute to a well-adjusted Cavalier that feels secure both in the presence and absence of their owners.

Changes in Routine: Sudden changes in the daily patterns or significant life events, such as moving to a new home or changing family dynamics, can increase anxiety in dogs.

Previous Negative Experiences: Dogs with a history of negative experiences may be more prone to separation anxiety.

Proven Strategies for Managing Separation Anxiety (For severe cases, consult a certified trainer.)

Gradual Desensitization: Initiate the process by leaving your Cavalier alone for brief periods, gradually extending the duration over time. This approach helps the dog acclimate to your absence, reducing anxiety. At first, the duration should be so brief that the dog doesn't even have the chance to get upset before you return. You should always aim to keep the dog under threshold. If done right, your dog progresses at a pace that doesn't stress them out enough to display serious distress signals. That being said, some dogs may whine a bit and then settle themselves down.

Safe Space Establishment: Designate a comfortable and secure area in your home where your Cavalier can stay when you're away. Enhance the space with toys, treats, and familiar scents to create an inviting environment. (Reference crate training for additional guidance.) A good tip is to close any shades/blinds and use a noise machine/TV to drown out outside noise. You can also look into crate covers. We don't want the dog to a) be triggered by a car door shutting or other dogs barking or b) feel like they have to guard the house. Furthermore, being in a crate tells the dog they do not need to keep a secure perimeter/guard the house. Their only job is to relax.

Counter-conditioning: Associate your departures with positive experiences. Offer treats or toys before leaving and avoid excessive excitement upon your return. This helps your dog perceive your absence as a neutral or positive event. Lickimats and frozen kongs are great for this. If your dog knows that crate time means a tasty peanut butter mat, then they will be excited for it.

2. Managing Excessive Barking

While barking is a natural form of canine communication, persistent barking can disrupt the peace and create tension with neighbors and family members. Employing proper training techniques and addressing the underlying causes can effectively control and reduce excessive barking in your Cavalier King Charles Spaniel.

Identifying Triggers

Attention-seeking: Some Cavaliers may bark excessively to gain attention from their owners.

Fear or Anxiety: Barking can serve as a coping mechanism for dogs experiencing fear or anxiety in specific situations.

Alerting: Cavaliers may bark to alert their owners to potential threats or unfamiliar stimuli.

Boredom/Lack of Enrichment/Lack of Exercise: Insufficient mental stimulation or physical activity can contribute to excessive barking.

Proven Techniques to Reduce Excessive Barking

Obedience Training: Teaching your Cavalier basic commands like "Quiet" or "Enough" can help them understand when barking is inappropriate. Consistent training is essential for success.

Exercise and Mental Stimulation: Regular daily exercise and mental enrichment activities will help alleviate boredom and reduce excessive barking.

Positive Reinforcement: Reward your Cavalier when they stop barking on command or remain calm in situations that typically trigger barking.

Environmental Management

Blocking Visual Triggers: Limit your Cavalier's access to areas where they can see or hear stimuli that trigger excessive barking, such as passing pedestrians or other animals. Frosted cling film for windows works wonders. You should restrict access to furniture near windows too.

White Noise: In some cases, providing white noise or calming music can help mask external sounds and reduce barking. Alexa has a setting that can play calming music when it hears your dog bark.

3. Managing Leash Pulling

Leash pulling is a common issue encountered during walks with Cavalier King Charles Spaniels. While it may be frustrating, addressing leash pulling is essential for the dog's safety and the enjoyable walking experience.

Loose Leash Walking

Teach your Cavalier to walk on a loose leash by offering rewards when they walk calmly beside you. If they begin to pull, halt until the leash becomes slack.

Employ positive reinforcement to acknowledge your Cavalier for walking politely on the

leash. High-value treats, praise, and affection serve as the best motivators in reinforcing desired behavior.

Utilizing Appropriate Gear

Front Clip Harness: Consider using a front clip harness designed to redirect your dog's attention toward you if they attempt to pull. This harness proves beneficial in curtailing leash pulling. Opt for a flat leash over retractable leashes when training your dog to maintain better control and communication. Flat leashes provide consistent tension and allow for clear signals, facilitating effective training and ensuring the safety of you and your dog. Additionally, it is important to remember to refrain from using choke chains or prongs. These harsh tools can cause discomfort, injury, and can have detrimental effects on a dog's well-being. Humane and effective training methods that prioritize the safety and comfort of your canine companion are always the best approach.

Consistency and Patience

Leash pulling can take time to improve, so be patient and consistent with your training efforts. Avoid harsh corrections, which may increase your dog's anxiety or frustration.

As loving and devoted companions, Cavalier King Charles Spaniels deserve the best care and understanding when addressing behavioral issues like separation anxiety, excessive barking, and leash pulling. By identifying the root causes of these problems and employing proven training techniques, you can help your Cavalier overcome these obstacles and develop a more balanced demeanor.

Remember that training requires time, patience, and consistency. Harsh punishments or neglecting to address behavioral issues may exacerbate the problem or lead to new challenges. Instead, foster a positive and supportive environment, using positive reinforcement to reinforce desired behaviors and encourage a more confident and well-adjusted Cavalier.

8　Fun and Enrichment Activities

Training your Cavalier King Charles Spaniel is not just about discipline; it's an opportunity to bond and create lasting memories with your loving companion. Incorporating fun and enrichment activities into your training routine will keep your Cavalier mentally stimulated and physically active, leading to a happier and well-trained dog. This chapter provides a comprehensive guide to different enjoyable activities and games you can engage in with your Cavalier, enhancing your relationship and ensuring your dog's overall well-being.

Fetch and Retrieve Games

Cavalier King Charles Spaniels have an instinct for retrieving, making fetch an ideal game to engage their hunting and retrieving skills. For indoor or outdoor fetch sessions, you can use balls, frisbees, or soft toys. To add a fun twist, incorporate basic obedience commands such as "Sit," "Stay," or "Come" while playing. This helps reinforce their training while enjoying the activity.

Puzzle Toys and Treat Dispensers

Mental stimulation is just as important as physical exercise for a Cavalier. Puzzle toys and treat dispensers challenge their problem-solving abilities and keep them mentally engaged. Fill these toys with treats or kibble, encouraging your dog to learn how to access the reward. Snuffle mats are great for this!

Hide-and-Seek

This classic game is not only enjoyable for kids but also for dogs. Hide-and-seek can be played indoors or outdoors. Have a family member or friend hold your Cavalier while you find a hiding spot. Then call out their name and let them use their keen sense of smell to locate you. Once they see you, celebrate with praise and treats, making it a rewarding experience for your dog.

Agility Training

Creating a mini-agility course in your backyard is an excellent method to engage and stimulate your Cavalier's physical and mental capacities. Incorporate items such as cones, tunnels, jumps, and weave poles. Guide your dog through the course using treats and positive reinforcement, fostering confidence and enhanc-

ing coordination. While dog parks are generally not recommended due to potential safety and health concerns, a group agility class could offer a more controlled and supervised environment for your Cavalier to enjoy and excel in agility training.

Nose Work

Cavalier King Charles Spaniels showcase remarkable sniffing abilities, making them ideal for engaging in nose work activities. Generate scent trails by strategically placing treats or their favorite toy in different locations around the house or yard. Stimulate your dog's sense of smell and reward them when they successfully locate the hidden items. Nose work not only taps into their natural instincts but also offers valuable mental stimulation. Consider exploring nose work classes, which are increasingly available and provide excellent opportunities for your Cavalier to further develop their olfactory skills.

Swimming

Many Cavaliers enjoy water activities, so if you can access a pool, dog friendly lake, or beach, take your pup for a swim. Swimming is a low-impact exercise that's gentle on their joints, making it suitable for dogs of all ages. Always supervise your dog around water and use a doggy life jacket if needed, especially if they are not confident swimmers.

Playdates and Dog Parks

Cavaliers flourish through socialization, benefiting from their naturally friendly and sociable disposition. Organize dedicated playdates for your Cavalier, allowing them to interact with diverse dog breeds and personalities. This practice not only refines their communication skills but also reduces the risk of potential behavioral issues in the future. It's advisable to opt for private playdates instead of public parks, considering the safety concerns associated with dog parks, such as health risks and hazards. As an alternative, consider engaging in pack walks with a trainer, which are particularly beneficial for dogs needing additional support in developing social skills.

Obedience Games

Turn obedience training into a game by introducing new challenges and increasing the difficulty level gradually. For example, have your Cavalier stay in a Sit or Down position for an extended period or teach them new tricks like

Rollover or High-five Games like Simon Says can be adapted for dogs and enhance their response to your commands.

Freestyle Dancing

If you have a playful and outgoing Cavalier, freestyle dancing can be enjoyable. Create a dance routine with your dog, incorporating tricks and movements set to music. Freestyle dancing strengthens the bond between you and your pup and provides a creative outlet for training. Cues like Spin, Back Up, Bow, and leg weaving made for great dance moves.

Treat Hunt

Establish a scavenger hunt by strategically hiding treats or toys in various locations within your home or yard. Prompt your Cavalier to employ their keen sense of smell and instincts to uncover these hidden treasures. This engaging activity stimulates their senses and aligns with their natural foraging tendencies, providing mental stimulation and promoting focus. Introduce the cue "Find It" to enhance communication during this interactive and enriching exercise. A quick and easy way to do this is to toss a handful of kibble onto the grass.

DIY Obstacle Course

Build a do-it-yourself (DIY) obstacle course using items you have at home, like cardboard boxes, hula hoops, and cushions. Guide your Cavalier through the system, rewarding them for each successful maneuver. This is a cost-effective and fun way to keep them physically active and mentally engaged.

Road Trips and Hiking

Cavaliers are excellent companions for road trips and outdoor escapades. Going on hikes or nature walks with them provides an opportunity to discover new scents and environments. Ensure your dog is securely leashed, and don't forget to pack water and snacks for both of you. Incorporating seatbelts attached to a harness, not a collar, is essential for safety during travel. Hiking not only offers abundant physical exercise but also serves as a wonderful occasion to strengthen your bond. A long leash is helpful so the dog can explore but still be under control.

Brain Games Group Classes

Starting training sessions with your Cavalier King Charles Spaniel is not just an enjoyable endeavor for both of you but it's an enriching one too. Be sure to include a variety of entertaining activities and games to ensure that your dog remains mentally stimulated and physically active. Whether it's a lively game of fetch, exploring puzzle toys, engaging in agility training, or trying out nose work, there's a wide array of exciting options to captivate your Cavalier's instincts and enhance their abilities. For added enrichment and socialization, consider joining brain games group classes, offering a fun and interactive environment for your dog to learn and interact with fellow canine friends.

Remember, a happy and well-trained dog only comes from the time and effort invested in their training and care. Make training sessions positive and rewarding, always using positive reinforcement techniques. With patience, consistency, and lots of love, you'll create lasting memories with your Cavalier, fostering a strong bond that will last a lifetime.

9 Health and Wellness

A healthy and happy Cavalier is more receptive to training and learning. This chapter explores the essential canine health and wellness aspects that every responsible dog owner should know. From proper nutrition and exercise to grooming tips and regular veterinary check-ups, we'll provide the knowledge to ensure your dog enjoys a long and vibrant life.

Nutrition and Diet

Proper nutrition is essential for the well-being of Cavalier King Charles Spaniels. This comprehensive guide will delve into the significance of tailoring their diet to factors such as age, activity level, and specific health requirements while also exploring the importance of feeding schedules, portion control, and the benefits of high-quality dog food. A well-balanced diet ensures they receive the essential nutrients, vitamins, and minerals required for proper growth, maintenance, and immunity. A healthy diet helps support their heart health, bone development, cognitive function, and shiny coat, which is characteristic of this breed.

Catering to Age, Activity Level, and Health Requirements

Just like humans, the nutritional needs of Cavalier King Charles Spaniels change as they age. Puppies have different dietary requirements than adult dogs, and senior Cavaliers may benefit from specialized diets to address age-related concerns. Consulting with a veterinarian is best to determine the best diet for each life stage.

It's important to take into account the activity level of Cavalier King Charles Spaniels when formulating their diet. More active dogs may necessitate a higher calorie intake to sustain their energy levels, whereas less active or senior dogs benefit from controlled portions to prevent weight gain and obesity. Obesity can lead to various health issues, including joint pain, reduced mobility, and an increased risk of other conditions, underscoring the importance of maintaining a balanced and appropriate diet tailored to their activity levels.

Addressing specific health requirements is another critical aspect of their diet. Cavaliers are not just prone to obesity; they are also at risk for health conditions like heart disease and dental issues too. Adjusting their diet to address these concerns can significantly impact their quality of life.

Feeding Schedules and Portion Control

A consistent feeding schedule benefits Cavaliers, as it helps regulate their metabolism and prevents overeating. Two meals a day are typically recommended for adult Cavaliers, while puppies may need three to four meals due to their higher energy demands. Avoiding free feeding, where food is left out all day, is essential to prevent excessive eating and weight gain.

Portion control is equally important. Overfeeding can lead to obesity, joint problems, and other health issues. On the other hand, underfeeding can result in malnutrition and insufficient energy levels. Consulting with a veterinarian can help determine the appropriate portion sizes based on the dog's age, weight, and activity level.

The Benefits of High-Quality Dog Food

Investing in high-quality dog food is one of the best choices owners can make for their Cavalier King Charles Spaniel. Premium dog food is specifically formulated to meet the dietary needs of different breeds, and it undergoes rigorous testing to ensure it contains the necessary nutrients. Look for dog food that lists meat as the primary ingredient, as Cavaliers require a protein-rich diet to support their energetic lifestyle.

Avoiding low-quality or generic dog food is essential, as these products often contain fillers, artificial additives, and excessive amounts of grains that offer little nutritional value to dogs. High-quality dog food may be more expensive, but it pays off in the long run by promoting better health and potentially reducing veterinary expenses.

The Role of Fresh Foods and Supplements

While high-quality dog food forms the basis of a Cavalier's diet, fresh foods can complement their meals. Small amounts of cooked meats, vegetables, and fruits can provide additional nutrients and add variety to their diet. However, avoiding certain foods toxic to dogs—such as chocolate, grapes, and onions—is essential.

Supplements can be beneficial in some cases, but they should only be administered under the guidance of a veterinarian. Giving unnecessary supplements may lead to nutrient imbalances, so it's important to identify specific deficiencies or health concerns before adding any supplements to the diet.

Your Cavalier deserves the best care, and a balanced and nutritious diet is central to their well-being. Tailoring their diet to their age, activity level, and specific health requirements ensures they lead a healthy and happy life. Establishing a consistent feeding schedule, controlling portions, and investing in high-quality dog food is vital to maintaining their overall health and vitality. Owners can show their love and commitment to these charming and affectionate dogs by providing proper nutrition.

Exercise and Playtime

Cavalier King Charles Spaniels are a breed characterized by their charming appearance and affectionate temperament. Behind their endearing expressions lies an energetic, playful spirit that craves physical activity. Originally bred as hunting dogs, they have maintained their love for being active and participating in various outdoor pursuits. However, in modern times, many Cavaliers primarily serve as beloved family pets, so it's best to cater to their inherent need for exercise and play.

Regular physical activities keep these adorable companions physically fit and provide essential mental stimulation, promoting their overall well-being. In this article, we will explore the benefits of exercise and play for Cavaliers, suggesting various activities and exercise routines that can keep them engaged and prevent boredom-related behavioral issues.

Like all dogs, they require opportunities to burn off excess energy and maintain a healthy weight, preventing obesity-related health issues. Regular exercise also supports cardiovascular health, muscle development, and joint mobility, promoting a longer and happier life.

Beyond physical benefits, exercise provides Cavaliers with vital mental stimulation. Mental enrichment prevents boredom and associated behavioral issues, such as excessive barking, chewing, or digging. A well-exercised Cavalier is more likely to be content, focused, and better behaved, making the human-canine bond even more enjoyable.

Pet Insurance

Pet insurance also plays a role in responsible Cavalier King Charles Spaniel ownership. These dogs, like any other breed, may encounter unexpected health issues or accidents throughout their lives. Having a comprehensive pet insurance plan ensures that your Cavalier receives prompt and necessary medical attention without causing financial strain. Regular veterinary check-ups, vaccinations, and potential emergencies become more manageable when covered by insurance, allowing pet owners to prioritize their dog's well-being without worrying about the associated costs. By investing in pet insurance, responsible owners can provide their Cavaliers with the best possible healthcare, ensuring a long, happy, and healthy life for their beloved furry family members.

Grooming and Care

This breed's luxurious and flowing coat requires proper maintenance to keep it in top condition and ensure the dog's overall health and hygiene. Regular grooming routines—including brushing, bathing, ear cleaning, dental care, and nail trimming—are essential to maintain this charming breed's impeccable appearance and well-being.

Brushing

You can keep the Cavalier King Charles Spaniel's coat looking its best with regular brushing. The breed's long, silky hair can quickly become tangled and matted, leading to discomfort and skin issues if not properly attended to. To prevent this, owners should brush their Cavalier's coat at least two to three times a week, using a soft-bristled or slicker brush. This removes loose hair and debris and distributes natural oils, giving the coat its characteristic sheen and promoting a healthy skin condition.

Bathing

Bathing the Cavalier King Charles Spaniel should be done as needed, typically every four to six weeks or whenever the dog gets dirty or smelly. It's essential to use a mild, dog-specific shampoo to avoid irritating sensitive skin. Owners should be gentle and thorough when bathing and rinse all the shampoo thoroughly to prevent residue buildup. Towel drying is recommended, followed by blow-drying on a low and cool setting if necessary. Extreme heat can damage the coat, so air drying is preferable.

Ear Cleaning

Due to their long, droopy ears, Cavaliers are susceptible to ear infections, as these ears can trap moisture and debris. Therefore, consistent ear cleaning is needed for proper ear hygiene. Owners should conduct weekly inspections and delicately wipe the ears using a damp cotton ball or a vet-approved ear cleaner to eliminate any accumulated buildup. It is important not to insert anything into the ear canal to prevent injury. If there are indications of redness, swelling, discharge, or additional signs like odor, excessive head shaking, or scratching, consulting a veterinarian promptly is essential.

Dental Care

Proper dental care is necessary for any dog, and Cavaliers are no exception. Their teeth should

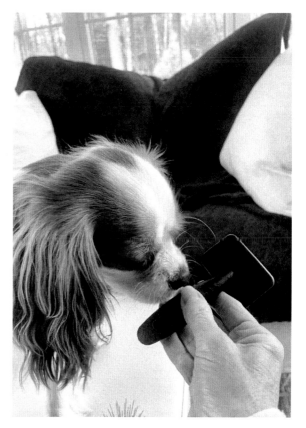

be brushed daily using a dog-specific toothbrush and toothpaste to prevent plaque buildup, tartar, and gum disease. Providing dental treats or toys that promote oral health can also be beneficial. Regular dental check-ups with a veterinarian are essential to promptly address any potential dental issues. Dental health also relates to heart health which can be a big issue for Cavaliers.

Nail Trimming

Regular nail trimming ensures the comfort of the Cavalier King Charles Spaniel and prevents overgrowth, which may lead to pain and difficulty in walking. Owners should trim their dog's nails every few weeks, being cautious not to cut into the quick, the sensitive part of the nail containing blood vessels and nerves. If uncertain about the proper technique, seek guidance from a professional groomer or your veterinarian.

Cavaliers boast a beautiful, silky coat, undoubtedly one of its most captivating features. However, maintaining it in top condition requires consistent grooming practices, including brushing, bathing, and ear cleaning, to prevent tangles, mats, and ear infections. Dental care and nail trimming should not be overlooked, as they contribute to impeccable hygiene and overall health.

Devoting time to the care of the Cavalier King Charles Spaniel's coat and hygiene enhances its appearance and also provides even more love and attention that these dogs crave, which ensures a healthy, happy, and impeccably groomed Cavalier for now and for years to come.

Preventative Healthcare

Preventative healthcare is the cornerstone of keeping your Cavalier King Charles Spaniel healthy and free from common ailments. These dogs deserve the best care possible to ensure they live long, happy lives. Owners can save their companions from potential distress by being proactive in their healthcare and maintaining their well-being.

One of the most critical aspects of preventative healthcare is ensuring that your Cavalier King Charles Spaniel receives essential vaccinations. Vaccinations protect dogs from contagious and potentially life-threatening diseases. Puppies should receive their initial series of vaccines starting at around six to eight weeks of age. Core vaccinations, vital for all dogs, include rabies, distemper, parvovirus, and canine adenovirus. Regular booster shots are necessary to maintain immunity throughout their lives.

Another aspect of preventative healthcare is managing parasites. Cavaliers, like all dogs, are vulnerable to pests like fleas, ticks, and internal worms. Fleas and ticks can result in skin irritations, anemia, and the transmission of diseases. On the other hand, intestinal worms may cause digestive problems and compromise the dog's overall health. It's imperative to apply preventive measures, such as regular topical treatments, oral medications, and collars specifically designed for parasite control, consistently and under a veterinarian's guidance. These actions are essential to safeguard the well-being of the Spaniel.

Regular veterinary check-ups are vital for detecting and addressing health issues early on. These routine visits allow veterinarians to monitor the Cavalier's overall health, identify developing health problems, and provide appropriate recommendations. During these visits, the vet

will perform a thorough physical examination, update vaccinations, and discuss any necessary lifestyle changes, dietary adjustments, or supplements that may benefit the dog's specific needs.

Preventative healthcare not only focuses on physical health but also includes mental and emotional well-being. Cavaliers are known for their affectionate and social nature and thrive on companionship. Regular exercise, mental stimulation, and spending quality time with their owners contribute to their overall happiness and overall contentment.

Owners can take proactive measures to prevent several common health issues associated with the breed. Regrettably, mitral valve disease (MVD) and syringomyelia, a condition characterized by fluid filled cavities within the spinal cord near the brain, are prevalent hereditary conditions in Cavaliers. Although these conditions cannot be entirely prevented, early detection and consistent monitoring can aid in managing their requirements and ensuring the best possible care for affected dogs.

Preventative healthcare maintains the health and happiness of your Cavalier King Charles Spaniel. Essential vaccinations protect them from dangerous diseases, while parasite control measures keep them free from external and internal parasites. Regular veterinary check-ups detect potential health issues early on, and proper grooming and weight management contribute to their overall well-being. Being proactive in their healthcare saves potential distress, ensuring these beautiful dogs thrive and enjoy a wonderful quality of life. As responsible pet owners, we must provide them with the best care possible, and preventative healthcare is a vital part of achieving that goal.

10 Training for Specific Roles

Beyond their role as loyal and loving pets, Cavaliers possess a versatile and adaptable nature that allows them to excel in various roles and activities. From therapy work to agility and obedience competitions, their intelligence, gentle demeanor, and eagerness to please make them an excellent fit for these specialized tasks. Cavaliers can thrive in different roles, and recognizing their unique talents will help them shine in their chosen fields.

Therapy Work

One of the most valuable roles Cavaliers can take on is that of a therapy dog. Their gentle and empathetic nature makes them perfect candidates for providing comfort, emotional support, and companionship. Therapy dogs are commonly found in hospitals, nursing homes, schools, and other facilities where their presence can positively impact the well-being of patients, residents, and students.

When training a Cavalier for therapy work, focusing on their natural ability to connect with people and remain calm in various situations is essential. Advanced obedience training ensures the dog can follow commands and exhibit appropriate behavior in different environments. Socialization is equally essential, as therapy dogs must be comfortable and confident when encountering new places, faces, sounds, and people.

Additionally, teaching the Cavalier specific cues such as "Sit," "Stay," "Leave It," and

"Down" is beneficial during therapy sessions. Introducing them to various surfaces, handling them gently, and exposing them to medical equipment helps prepare them for encounters in hospitals and healthcare facilities. A therapy dog must also be comfortable being touched and hugged, as physical contact is a very important part of that role.

Agility

Cavalier King Charles Spaniels may not be the first breed that comes to mind when thinking of agility competitions, but they can surprise many with their athleticism and eagerness to participate. Agility is an exciting and challenging sport that involves navigating an obstacle course in a set order within a specific time frame.

Cavaliers must undergo rigorous training to learn to jump, weave through poles, navigate tunnels, and traverse various surfaces to excel in agility. Since Cavaliers are not a very large or heavy breed, agility training should be adjusted to prevent injuries and strain on their joints.

Positive reinforcement and clicker training are excellent methods for teaching agility skills to Cavaliers. By breaking down the obstacles into smaller steps and gradually increasing the difficulty, Cavaliers can build confidence and enjoy the training process. Remember that patience and consistency are key when training a Cavalier for agility, as it may take some time for them to grasp the intricacies of the sport.

Obedience Competitions

A Cavalier's desire to please their owners makes them fantastic candidates for obedience competitions. These competitions test a dog's ability to follow commands, respond promptly, and maintain focus in distracting environments.

Begin obedience training early in a Cavalier's life, starting with basic cues like "Sit," "Stay," "Come," and "Heel." Positive reinforcement, reward-based training, and short, regular training sessions work best with this breed. Cavaliers are sensitive dogs and respond positively to praise and treats when they do well.

Gradually increase the complexity of cues and add distractions to prepare them for competition settings. Consistency in training and clear communication between the dog and handler are essential for success in obedience competitions.

Recognizing a Cavalier's Unique Talents and Passions

To bring out the best in a Cavalier, you need to discern their distinctive talents and passions. While they are generally affectionate and eager to please, each dog may have individual inclinations and preferences for how they want to spend their time.

Observe Their Interests

Pay attention to the actions and environments that your Cavalier finds most enjoyable. Some may show a natural inclination towards agility, while others might demonstrate exceptional calmness and sensitivity, making them suitable for therapy work. By observing their responses during different engagements, you can more accurately assess where their talents lie.

Positive Reinforcement

Positive reinforcement is key when encouraging Cavaliers to pursue their chosen role. Reward them with praise, treats, and affection when they show interest or excel in a particular activity. This positive feedback reinforces their behavior and strengthens the bond between you and your dog.

Be Patient and Flexible

Not every Cavalier will excel in every role, and that's okay. Be patient with your dog as they explore different activities, and adjust your training methods accordingly. If they show little interest in a particular activity, consider trying something that aligns better with their personality and abilities.

Consider Professional Guidance

If you're uncertain about which role would suit your Cavalier best or how to proceed with specialized training, consider seeking guidance from professional trainers with experience with the breed and the specific activities you're interested in pursuing.

Cavaliers have the potential to excel in various specialized roles, ranging from therapy work, where their gentle demeanor brings comfort, to agility and obedience competitions, where their intelligence and eagerness to please shine. Recognizing your Cavalier's unique talents and passions and tailoring their training accordingly will enable them to thrive and reach their full potential in their chosen role. Whether it's spreading joy to patients in hospitals, conquering agility courses with enthusiasm, or showcasing their obedience skills in competitions, Cavaliers have the heart and spirit to make a lasting impact in the lives of everyone they meet.

11   The Aging Cavalier King Charles Spaniel

As beloved companions, Cavalier King Charles Spaniels bring immeasurable joy to their owners throughout their lives. As they grow older, pet parents need to adapt to their changing needs and abilities to ensure they continue to enjoy life to the fullest. Like humans, aging affects dogs in various ways, leading to physical, cognitive, and emotional alterations in their lives. This chapter will explore adjusting training routines and activities, supporting their health, and providing the best care possible during their golden years.

Understanding the Aging Process

As Cavaliers age, they experience a range of physical and behavioral changes. Their once boundless energy gradually diminishes, making them less active and more susceptible to stiffness and joint issues. Cognitive decline may also occur, resulting in memory lapses and alterations in behavior. In addition to the common signs of aging, such as decreased mobility, increased sleeping hours, graying of the muzzle, diminished hearing, and reduced vision, increased

anxiety or restlessness can also be part of this process too.

If your dog becomes aggressive in its old age, consult a vet or trainer.

Adapting Training Routines and Activities

Exercise

While regular exercise remains a priority for overall health, tailoring the intensity and duration to suit your aging Cavalier's capabilities is essential. Gentle walks and low-impact activities can help maintain muscle tone and joint flexibility without overexertion. Swimming short distances is a joint-friendly option.

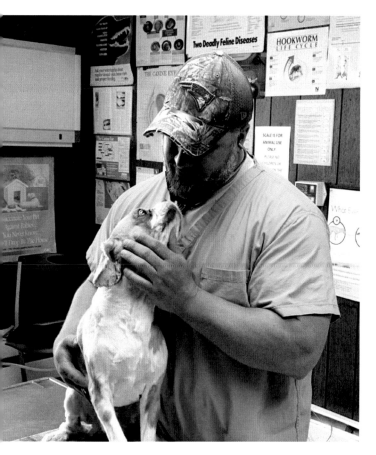

Mental Stimulation

Cognitive exercises are vital to keep an aging Cavalier's mind sharp. Engage in interactive games, puzzle toys, and short training sessions focusing on mental stimulation rather than physical exertion.

Training Patience

Aging can bring about slower responses and decreased attention span. Be patient during training sessions and avoid frustration. Use positive reinforcement and rewards to encourage desired behaviors.

Supporting Health in the Golden Years

Nutrition

As dogs age, their metabolism changes, and they may require adjustments in their diet. Consult your veterinarian to determine the best senior dog food that meets their nutritional needs. High-quality, easily digestible food can help maintain a healthy weight and support joint health.

Weight Management

Obesity can exacerbate senior Cavaliers' joint issues and other health problems. Monitor their weight closely and adjust their diet and exercise to prevent excess weight gain.

Regular Vet Check-ups

Regular visits to the veterinarian become even more critical in a dog's senior years. Semi-annual check-ups can help detect health issues early and ensure appropriate interventions.

Dental Care

Dental health is vital to a dog's overall well-being. Dental problems are common in older dogs, so it's important to always remember regular dental check-ups and dental hygiene practices too.

Joint Health

Veterinarian-prescribed joint supplements can contribute to maintaining optimal joint health and easing discomfort related to arthritis or other joint conditions. Explore options such as physical therapy or specialized therapies like hydrotherapy to address specific joint issues too.

Comfort and Environment

Cozy Bedding

Provide your aging Cavalier with a soft, supportive, and easily accessible bed to relieve pressure on their joints. Orthopedic beds can be particularly beneficial.

Climate Control

Older dogs are more sensitive to temperature extremes. Ensure a comfortable environment with appropriate heating or cooling as needed.

Assistance with Mobility

Ramps or steps can help your Cavalier easily access furniture or vehicles. Avoid situations that require excessive jumping or climbing. Carpets and rugs may help a dog that is nervous on slippery floors.

Regular Grooming

Older Cavaliers may have difficulty grooming themselves. Regular grooming sessions can help maintain their coat's health and prevent matting.

Emotional Support

Maintain Routine

Stick to a consistent daily routine, as changes can cause stress or confusion in older dogs.

Patience and Understanding

Be understanding of any changes in behavior or temperament. Senior dogs may need more reassurance and comfort during this phase of their life.

Quality Time Together

Spend quality time with your aging Cavalier, engaging in low-key activities they enjoy. This bond will help reduce anxiety and promote emotional well-being.

Providing the best care for an aging Cavalier King Charles Spaniel involves a mix of physical adjustments, emotional support, and regular veterinary care. By adapting training routines and activities to suit their changing needs, supporting their health through proper nutrition and medical attention, and creating a comfortable and loving environment, pet owners can ensure their beloved companions enjoy their golden years to the fullest. The unconditional love and loyalty these wonderful dogs provide throughout their lives deserve the utmost care and respect as they gracefully age by our side.

Conclusion

This book was written to serve as a valuable resource throughout your training journey, offering techniques and advice to navigate challenges. As you explore its pages, may you find inspiration and guidance tailored to your Cavalier's unique personality and needs. Training is a continual adventure requiring patience, consistency, and positive reinforcement. Embrace each step, for through these efforts, you and your Cavalier will build a strong, loving bond.

Training instills obedience and reinforces the connection between you and your Cavalier. It's an opportunity to understand your dog's behavior, preferences, and communication cues, fostering a happy relationship. Maintain a positive attitude and patience, adjusting to your pet's pace, and prioritize consistency with short, engaging sessions scheduled regularly.

Remember the power of positive reinforcement—through treats, praise, and affection—to reward desired behaviors, avoiding punishment-based techniques to preserve trust. Socialization is integral; expose your Cavalier to diverse environments, people, and animals early on to build confidence and good manners, reducing the risk of behavioral issues.

Anticipate challenges and setbacks, but persistence is key. Seek support from communities, trainers, or fellow dog owners if needed. Training is an ongoing process; regularly reinforce skills and introduce new challenges. Care for your Cavalier's overall well-being with a balanced diet, exercise, and veterinary check-ups.

As your journey unfolds, treasure the memories and adventures you share. May this book continue to serve as a guiding light in your training endeavors. Embrace the joy and challenges of training and may your bond with your Cavalier grow stronger each day. I wish you both many years of happiness, love, and cherished memories together. Happy training!

—*Christine*

About the Author

Passionate about Cavaliers, Christine has dedicated decades to her love for the breed, serving as a devoted hobby breeder and engaging in various Cavalier-exclusive endeavors. As the author of *The Complete Cavalier Compendium: A Guide to Loving and Understanding Your Cavalier King Charles Spaniel* and *Knox and Charlie Go to England*, Christine's commitment to sharing her knowledge and affection for Cavaliers shines through. Her latest venture, *Knox and Charlie: The Superhero Dog*, marks the second installment in her series of children's books inspired by the Cavalier King Charles Spaniel breed.

Made in United States
Orlando, FL
07 January 2025

57006209R00033